Seasons of Healing

M. Gail Grant

ISBN-13: 978-1-73-588755-5

Table of Contents

Seasonal Rejuvenation

The seasons whisper

renewed life

into my soul.

As the weariness

of each quarter

begins to weigh heavy,

and the aches and pains

of life intensify,

the last breaths of the season

quietly pass by,

and renewal of

faith, love, and strength

swiftly rush in.

Stillness

When life becomes

consuming,

and the days are filled

with anxiety and stress,

remove yourself

from it all,

seeking refuge

in the hidden wilderness,

where the sounds

and silence

of nature

will fulfill your

only needs.

Rings of Life

The seasons of life

mimic the rings of a tree,

displaying our growth.

Renewed Perceptions

Adults tend to complicate

their lives,

building financial wealth

and expanding responsibilities

to the outer rims

of society's projected expectations.

As you smother

and begin to suffocate,

re-evaluate the meaning

of

it all.

Murky Water

The older I get,

the clearer that I can see

through murky water.

Instinctual Awareness

Instinct is an innate trait

that we are

born with,

that by nature,

protects our soul.

If you feel

the constraints

of life's work

is like flying into the headwinds

of a catastrophic storm,

your instincts may be

desperately trying

to tell you

to wait

out

the downpour.

Broken Promises

The fire in my soul

burns stronger than your broken

promises can hurt.

Crying Souls

Anxiety within our souls

stems from

the inner voice

screaming to be heard.

Yet,

most of us carry on,

ignoring the crying

and urging

of our inner-most

thoughts,

begging us for just a moment

to

be

heard.

Peaceful Pathways

Forgiveness is the

pathway to

eternal peace

and happiness.

No Vacancy

For so many years,

I let life's responsibilities

drink from

my

inner-self,

and for so many years,

thereafter,

I felt empty

and

alone.

Once I turned the sign around

to now show *'closed,'*

I quickly realized

how easy it was

to refill

the glorious, internal

pot

of

gold.

Insecurities

A *'no'* may conjure

thoughts of inadequacies,

but stifle them quick.

A Bluebird's Message

The bluebirds circle

around me

during the ushering

of

early spring,

with flutters of perfectly defined,

feathered wings.

Their songs

rock my soul

as though

I am nestled warmly

inside their

carefully crafted nest,

reminding me

that life is the purpose —

not the broken mess.

Faithful Seeds

Unwavering faith

is the secret to success,

fulfilling all needs.

The Golden Fall

The golden shades

of the autumn

leaves

remind me

that no matter how

dark life seems

to be,

there has been,

and

will always be,

a golden light

to

embrace.

Insight

Disappointment may
allow opportunities
to shine in new light.

Natural Healing

The soul

will sing you a song

and dance

in the brisk winter breeze

as soon as you

step outside

and smell nature's

ingredients,

crafted as a recipe

to nourish and repair

just about

anything.

Commitment

Commitment breeds a
life of substance and purpose
beyond worldly ways.

Avalanche

When an avalanche

destroys the road up ahead,

view it as a gift.

Naturalistic Design

You can't bloom

in the spring

without

capturing the harvest

and

hibernating for rest.

All things are seasonal

in that

renewal is a direct

effect

of self-love

and

self-care.

Nature mirrors the lessons

that

we

forget.

Hateful Notions

Hate is a disguised
manifestation of self
insecurities.

Crossroads

All lives

lead to crossroads

in this journey

called life.

One road leads to

internal fulfillment

with happiness

as the prize.

The other road leads to

anger and hate,

traits that arise when

the mind

cancels the soul.

If it doesn't feel right,

it probably

never

was.

Purposeful Rhetoric

Understanding the

reasons behind the spoken

words build clarity.

Distorted View

The closer the view,

the more pixelated the

image will become.

Fuzzy Socks

My heart begins

skipping beats

when the colors of fall

begin to swirl

in the air,

and the sun begins to set

earlier

on the horizon,

urging me

to go inside

and cozy up

with my favorite pair

of fuzzy socks,

finding time

to enjoy life's little things.

Discernment

Watching from afar

gives valuable insight —

a clearer picture.

Warning: Detour

Your inner feelings

are the soul's only way of

warning to detour.

Lost Civilization

Love gets lost

in the commotion

of life

because

humanity

has decided

to value

tangible assets

over

togetherness.

Magnified Mistakes

The rearview mirror

has a way of simplifying

my greatest mistakes.

Societal Embrace

When I reflect

upon my most desperate of choices,

I find they occurred

as a direct effect

of a soul reaching out

for

warmth and grace.

Those around you

that seem lost

may be slowly drowning

from a loss of self-worth.

Go the extra step,

and show them that they matter,

for each one of us

innately begs

to be

accepted by others,

facilitating a universal oneness

with powers that can heal

beyond the depths of despair.

Miraculous Events

Stand tall when it rains

because through the raging storm

miracles are born.

Transparency

He read my poem

the other day

and commented on the

darkness in theme.

I let him know the

difference between him and me

was that

I am willing

to crack the surface,

exposing it all,

allowing the light

to shine

through

my brokenness.

Never be ashamed of

facing the forces

of negativity

that present in your life.

Healing.

Calculated Purpose

They say art is for

those preferring to daydream,

or is it clairvoyance?

Tapestry of Life

Self-expression and creativity

are elements of art

that paint life

around the soul.

Let the soul

live free

and

celebrate the tapestry

that comes to be.

Humanistic Work

The work that we choose
to devote our heart and soul
is our legacy.

Therefore, thoughtfully
consider your life's purpose
without salary.

Healthy Menu

If nature has a heartbeat,

and it relies upon

a healthy menu

to sustain life,

maybe we should spend

more time

sharing our

thoughts of

love.

Christian Living

Nature has a way
of reminding us to still
our minds and just pray.

Melodious Water

The sound of

water

must be

mathematically orchestrated

because as it flows

through

the creek,

the melody vibrates

through

my inner being.

A Bird's Goodbye

Whispering goodbye,

the birds fly in synchronized

formation up high.

Difficult Reflection

Carry a journal

with you

and

take note of your moods;

document your perceptions

of

why you feel the way you do

during these moments

of reflection.

Through healthy discernment,

you many find

your key to happier and healthier living.

If the results

disappoint you,

difficult decisions

may lie ahead.

But one thing is for sure —

life is way too short

to settle for anything less

then what is closest

to

your heart.

Cyclical Reminder

The seasons remind

us of death and renewal,

welcoming new blooms.

Happiness as a Choice

Unfortunately, there are

forces of evil

that surround us

every day.

Reaffirm your choices

by

verbally declaring them

as the only way.

You will find that evil

loves misery,

and the more you embrace happiness,

the more happiness will want to stay.

Inner Peace

Forgiveness is key

to a life of inner peace.

Embrace the challenge.

Innate Reminder

Sometimes the pressures

of life

seem to choke us,

causing distress and strife.

In the most difficult

of times,

do something that reminds

you of who you really are.

The mind

wants you to believe

that play is for the young,

but the heart will lead you

to your old

stomping ground,

where sheer happiness

will pull you by the hand,

welcoming a chance

to remind you

of the internal infrastructure that

you forgot

to protect.

Go ahead and dance,

basking in the feelings

of

yesterday.

Marriage Proposal

Marry me, he said,

for my heart is yours, alone,

until death summons.

Driver Seat

The one thing that

society

seems to stress

is that we as a people

are no longer free.

However,

this is the greatest lie

that will ever

exist

because nothing in this life

has the power

to manifest

a change in the

ethereal soul

unless

you decide

to

get into the

passenger

seat.

Timeless Grace

Thankful for His love
and gift of eternal life,
regardless of sin.

Look Within

Happiness and fulfillment

cannot be bought.

They are gifts

manifested from the willingness

to accept

and believe

that human nature is good,

something easy to sway

away from

when the tides of life

get high.

External forces

push a narrative that urges

one

not to comply,

but leaning on God-given

wisdom,

my friend,

will always provide.

Self-Comparison

Admiration sows

subliminal self-doubts of

worthlessness and shame.

Winter Reminders

Winter reminds us

that

there will be seasons

in our lives

to

rest and repair,

waiting for the newness

of

spring.

Mid-Life

In the middle of

life is where the path will fork,

allowing for change.

Seasonal Lessons

In the spring,

we softly bud and grow.

In the summer,

we reach full bloom.

In the fall,

we reflect upon our growth.

In the winter,

we rest and prepare to begin anew.

Be like the seasons,

providing yourself

an opportunity

to learn from your past,

celebrate your growth,

embrace changes and new perspectives,

and get excited

for what is

to

come.

Evolution of Time

Time itself doesn't heal
but by God's merciful grace
we glean perspective.

Influential Life

Think of all that you

have met,

that in some small way,

positively affected and influenced

your life.

As you are smiling

and enjoying the moment,

realize that your name

will appear

on someone else's

list.

Introspective Sessions

Spending hours daily
reflecting on the choices
made will mature minds.

Soul's Paradise

Nature

exudes

internal beauty

as much as it

provides

a visual window

to the

soul's

paradise.

Deep Reflection

Life lessons provide

moments of deep reflection,

strengthening results.

Bodyguard

You are the keeper

of your

own mind,

body,

and

soul.

Nothing gets in

without your consent.

Protect your oneness

as though

leeches

really do

exist.

Storm Clouds

Cold and dark gray skies
remind us of our resolve
to weather the storm.

Roadblocks of Grace

It seems that

when life

feels dramatically out of control,

it is tactics

such as these

that are used

by the soul

to cause us

to slow down

and

re-evaluate

what is best.

Maybe, what we

are pushing for

is not the best

at nourishing

inner-being

and

self-worth.

Tough Love

Sincere warmth disguised
as steadfast opposition
rejuvenates.

Vessel of Transportation

Change

is a part of life

that reminds us

of where we began,

where we've been,

and where we

still need to go.

Change

is a roadmap of

life

that pushes us

through the valleys,

over the mountain tops,

and into the river currents.

Just keep going.

Dire Times

The best life lessons

are those learned in the most

stark circumstances.

Progression

Stop and take a picture

of

where you are today.

Put it

in a drawer

for another day.

Months or years

down the road,

pull out the image and

now rejoice

of where

you

have arrived

at this moment in time.

Truthful Composition

The human body

harvests thoughts as visible

notions of the truth.

Transcendent Progress

When we don't

let sadness

and perceived failure

steal our

self-worth,

these attributes

will lead

to

significant

moments

of

transcendent progress.

Overnight

Tomorrow

is a way

of acknowledging

change

is just

one sleep

away.

Found Treasure

Sometimes,

treasures are

found

on the path

that is least

traversed.

Being unique

is a gift

of endless

worth.

Mindful Realization

Training the mind to
hear the soul is of utmost
priority in life.

Spiritual Underpinnings

Spirituality is defined

by the self.

Religion is a discourse

created by man.

Just because man

doesn't embrace it,

doesn't mean that

it doesn't exist.

Not everything in

life

must be

defined

or fit

into a categorical box.

Some of life's most

magnificent of gifts

cannot be touched —

only felt.

Close your eyes

and

open your

mind.

Forecasted

The future may be

unknown to thee, but to Him,

there's no mystery.

Powerful Disguise

Collective shaming

is a way of

guilting humanity

into supporting narratives

driven by powerful

people.

The question

that you must ask

yourself

is

why?

If I comply

and sin

against my sense of self,

what do *they* win?

Is the submission in and of itself

the only

mission?

Universal Connectedness

Breathe deep and accept

life as a gift to embrace

unified meaning.

Beyond the Surface

Be thankful for

every day

that

this beautiful

earth

provides.

Beauty may be realized

underneath

every over-turned

rock.

Looking at the

surface

only dulls

the

vision.

Fueling Happiness

Public servants give

of themselves in exchange for

peaceful exhaustion.

Tasty Food

Flowers,

birds,

and

trees

are the spices

in life.

Without their

presence,

the spiritual food

would

taste

bland.

Rememberings

Childhood has a way
of reminding the soul how
to receive a gift.

Spiritual Armor

In the depths of the forest

is where

the silence overwhelms

all external forces.

Surrounding yourself

with the protective armor

of nature

will leave your

spiritual enemy

trembling

in the knees.

Shared Misery

Evil vices of
miserable wallowing
induce painful shame.

Mindful Solutions

I have surrendered

to the idea

that living in

today's race

is extinguishing

my inner flame.

Changes are on the way.

Colorful Promise

In taking seconds

to display, rainbows remind

us of God's promise.

Linguistic Notions

If thoughts and feelings

came before language,

there is a chance

that the

soul communicated

within parameters of

it's own.

Maybe the

spiritual language

resides still

in the crevices

of the brain,

pushed aside

for modern language conventions.

Perhaps,

healing involves

reprioritizing modes

of

communication.

Replenishing Faith

Fill your watering can

to the brim, and feed your

faith generously.

Be Yourself

Go ahead

and

devour the cookie.

Life's simple

delights have more

meaning

than any

accolades.

Great joy comes from pleasure —

not climbing

society's

ladder of limiting expectations.

Self-Actualization

Conquer your greatest

insecurities and doubts

to emit pure light.

Nightlights

Darkness shouldn't scare you

because

you always have the ability

to simply turn

the light

on.

Meaningful Service

Our purpose is to help others

identify

their own self-worth.

Ironically,

we find meaning and contentment

when not focusing

on

ourselves.

Balanced Life

The ocean tides

slap against the shore,

reminding us that every moment of life

is equally balanced

with

continuous give and take.

Universal Truth

Good versus evil

is as old as humankind

yet relevant still.

Students

There is a kindness

and decency

that lives in nature.

As humans,

we have so much

to

learn.

Hidden Sanctuary

In the forest deep,

lives the manifestation

of living God's way.

Giving

Sharing your inner peace

with others

is a gift

that can't be beaten,

for calmness in the soul

drives

everything else.

Frequency of Life

The ability

to filter degrading noise

births new frequencies.

Earthly Pitfalls

I sit for hours

while the words

glide across the page,

wondering if anyone

out there

will learn from my mistakes

of ignoring

the lifeforce within

while focused on

unsuccessful praise.

Conformity

Climbing

the ladder of praise

will muzzle creative works

when the focus becomes

coloring

inside the lines

instead of blending the edges,

enhancing

the overall design.

Shared Experiences

You must learn

to love and appreciate yourself

before

you can expect to

feel successful in

relationships.

This includes learning to value

yourself

as an equal player.

Everyone

has previous life experiences

before they find each other.

Embrace the diverse wealth

of education and learning that

your peers

provide.

Uniquely You

Our attributes

define our uniqueness

through shared expressions.

Innocence Lost

The warmth of the sun

as it

dances across the

side of my face

reminds me of those

young childhood

ways

of

innocent play —

oh, how I miss

those

blissful

days.

Loneliness

Dark, brisk winter nights
invoke feelings of dread,
knowing you are gone.

Regrets

The short autumn days

leave me counting the ways

that your absence in my life

cuts through my soul,

a make-shift jagged blade,

manifesting a dismal haze

of deep sadness

that

feasts on my

inner thoughts.

It seems

corruption

of my mind

stems from the

loss of your

daily presence,

beckoning me

to

enjoy life.

Thankful and Redeemed

There is great relief
in joyful realization
of His salvation.

Recursive Connections

At times,

the cycle of life

is difficult to understand,

as new births and deaths

seem to represent one extreme to another.

For each new generation that prospers and grows,

another will graciously leave

with their imprints in someone's story.

All we have left

are the memories that reside

as visual images

in our brains,

but the magic that occurs

with a familiar scent or word,

will forever live inside

our

hearts.

Love is the Answer

Life is a lesson,

teaching grace and compassion,

so everyone loves.

Stolen Moments

Steal quiet moments

for yourself

throughout the day.

They don't have to be planned

or take place in a hidden space.

Simply close your eyes

and enjoy the escape

from the day's pressures

of the world.

Two minutes of focused healing

will literally

transform

the

journey.

Like Wildflowers

That which we nurture

will incessantly grow wild,

overcoming doubt.

Patiently Blooming

If you have ever planted flower seeds,

watered them,

and watched them grow,

then you already understand your

life's purpose.

When the flowers show

growth

and their petals burst open

in glory

for the world to see,

their purpose is exposed.

You see,

the flower was patient,

taking in all the necessary nutrients,

becoming resilient to the strong, gusty breezes,

waiting for the opportune moment

to bring beauty

and happiness

to someone else's life.

Take your time

and prepare

to

bloom.

Internal Demise

Cancerous of thoughts
will manifest wicked ways
of unholiness.

Forever Friend

Have that special

friend in your life

that will listen intently

when your world

is

falling apart,

who will wipe away your tears

and

love you through your pain,

but will always remind you

how much they need you

in

return.

Balance.

Chosen Family

Brothers and sisters

found through unity and grace

are my family.

Ambassador of Light

The holidays are

a special time of the year

when many like to reflect

on the course of the year,

committing to changes

or making peace with the past.

Remember,

not everyone has a family of their own

to share in the joy and laughter

of the sights and sounds.

Make it a point

to reach out and share

words of hope,

a kindness that will make a difference

for many feeling

sad and alone.

Open your heart to others,

for the joy you receive in return

will supersede the extra effort.

Diffusion

If what happens in
church expands outside those walls,
glory is abound.

Broken Hearts

Relationships come and go,

even the ones that we think

will last

our

lifetime.

Betrayal of the heart

is a condition that cannot heal

on humankind's own.

It requires a sense of peace and understanding

that only our God

can provide,

for man, alone, does not have the

wherewithal

to mend

such delicate and intimate pieces

of

our souls.

As the Bible references,

do not rely on your own knowledge.

Pray for healing and guidance.

Projection of Sin

Judgment of sin

is reserved for only Him,

yet others do try.

Emotional Abandonment

It is possible for two people

to remain married

and living in the same home,

not willing to admit

they had an emotional

divorce,

years ago.

Fractured Relationships

Growing apart may

result in splintered feelings,

a drifting away.

Begin – End – Repeat

Relationships are

like seasons in life.

They grow.

They bloom.

They blossom.

They wilt.

They die.

The difference is

whether or not

you continue to

water and fertilize

next year's seeds.

Earned Knowledge

Difficult seasons

facilitate superb growth

of the mindful soul.

Dulling the Pain

The older one becomes,

the more spirituality

rears its head.

For some,

this newfound element is exhilarating

and curiosity fuels each step forward.

For others,

the surprise is

unwelcomed

because it is much easier to feel numb

inside

then it is to

embrace

the awakening.

Confused Reality

There is a sad nuance

that cognitive dissonance

promotes, alone.

Spiritual Growth

The storms of life

are meant to strengthen

your mental and spiritual

resolve.

Accept them as

a necessary means

to learn more about yourself.

The storms will pass,

and the aftermath brings fresh

sunshine and harmony,

a renewed sense of self

with the ability to surpass previously

known strength.

Treasure Map

Failure is a gift

that morphs into a blueprint

of how to succeed.

Unmasking

Identity is something

that can change.

What we embrace

and align

ourselves with

may adapt to the spiritual growth

that we have been bestowed.

Others may fight the transition

because their own identity is woven into our own.

While the change may be difficult

and disappointment looms from all,

snap the constraints of falsehoods,

welcoming a greater connection

to your authentic self.

It's okay to make the change.

Labels and categorical elements

do not have the power

to resist

the

evolution.

Metacognitive Reflections

At some point in life,

the mind questions itself through

metacognition.

Strategic Moves

If you ever

truly wonder

how someone feels about you,

let them answer the question

when you are not around.

If you ever

truly wonder

how someone values your relationship,

watch from afar.

If the results feel disappointing,

realize the knowledge,

regardless of how difficult it may be,

is, ultimately, a gift

that will lead you to a much better

place.

Unwanted Realizations

I can count

on one hand

how many times that

I have been deeply hurt.

I just noticed

that you own

the

majority.

The Unknown

What if
is such an
overwhelming
notion.

Self-Commitment

Being true to your inner self

is one

of the most essential life lessons.

Besides your mother,

no one else will

have the same level of

commitment to

your happiness.

No matter how much

someone loves you,

never doubt the fact that, ultimately,

they love themselves too.

Microseconds

Life is crazy

in that sometimes

it only takes one small,

seemingly trivial moment

to cause a

derailment of

events.

Gravitational Quandary

Underpinnings of

the notion of gravity

challenge what we know.

Intuitive Hints

The soul offers

subtle hints

that act as gentle

nudges

when we need them

the most.

Pay attention.

Intuition.

Difficult Communication

For some, words remain

the most difficult of all

to humbly express.

Entanglement

They say,

love is one of the

greatest of joys

we can know.

As in most things

in this life,

there is a significant

entanglement of highs

and

lows.

Child of God

Glorified in Him,

forever I will remain

faithful in my heart.

Perceived Reality

When presented with insecurity,

be careful how you frame

the feelings to your

mind,

for how your mind

categorizes the emotion

may determine

your course of life.

Perceptions

become

reality.

Fearful Horizons

The unknown future
cultivates feelings of
fearful horizons.

Unfaithful in Spirit

I used to believe

that as long as

we were faithful

and true,

our sunset would

never dim.

You showed me

that unfaithfulness

often lies in

mental connections over time —

beyond the physical realms.

Broken Trust

Trust is difficult

to earn but quite simple to

eternally lose.

Divine Package

We often don't talk

about it,

but the most difficult

emotion

to understand and accept

is one of a negative shock.

It is almost as though

the human mind and soul

need a buffer

that slowly begins to prepare

the heart

for what's to come.

The crushing agony that arises

from the burning ashes

is difficult to overcome.

During times such as these,

nothing seems to soften the blow.

There is an internal peace

that, quite frankly,

only comes from above,

so open up

to the Lord above

for the divine package

to be received.

Conscious Connection

The heart and the mind

collaboratively work

to defend thyself.

Musings of Mid-Life

During the season

of young parenthood,

I forgot to include me.

Exhaustion and hurt are now

riding the mid-life waves.

Time Pressures

The essence of time

will fool a wise one into

giving up the goal.

Collective Weight

As a woman, wife, and mother,

I go around

collecting other's things

to include

hats, shoes, and clothes

left lying around —

abandoned for the time being.

What I never realized,

was how heavy the load

quickly becomes.

Maybe, my job isn't

to carry these things,

trying to sort them out.

Maybe, my job is to

teach others

to carry their own load,

leaving them enough space to

begin missing these things

when they need them close.

In other words,

as one person,

we are not meant

to carry the world

all on our own.

Individually,

we must love, learn, and grow,

providing others

a safe space

to become their own.

Let your load become lighter.

Your value as a person

is not defined

by the weight of the baggage

you carry around.

Allow others the opportunity

to learn

to carry

their

own.

Soulful Tears

I have observed

that unsettled

irritability

is

the result of

tears flowing

from the soul.

Denial

The ache from within

compels the human mind

to ignore the soul.

Energy of Life

Emotional ties

are a direct connection

of

energy flowing

between

two souls.

Collective Consciousness

The energy you

emit transforms another's

perception of life.

Energetic Exchange

The exchange

of physical and emotional energy

is continuous.

Be sure to evaluate

the

discrepancy of exchange

often.

Equality.

Medicinal Properties

.

The frequency one

unconsciously may absorb

alters mental states.

Careful Review

The seasons of perceptions

from birth till death

manifest

the evolution of

growth

one must

wholeheartedly engage,

for tomorrow's direction

is

greatly influenced

by the previous day.

New directions require focused attention.

Erase and Revise

Tomorrow hasn't been

written in permanent ink.

Revise as needed.

Projected Expectations

Your expectations

are so cumbersome

and expansive

that I can't quite

carry them

without breaking

my back.

Perhaps,

if I put them down

and

worry about my own,

my soul will heal

and lead me to

inner peace —

a place called home.

Authentic Love

True love will reside

between the knowledgeable

givers of the same.

Bandage Removal

Meditation,

at first,

is a scary thing

because its nature requires

one to search

within

for answers

that are already there

buried deep

within

the

security gates.

A Shining Light

Learning more about
oneself is unsettling as
surprises illuminate.

Avoiding Hurricanes

With every bit of sting that

I feel

as your true feelings and intentions

are revealed,

my soul takes one step away

from

tomorrow's blistering rain,

slowly walking away

from

impending pain.

Walk Away

Desperation of

another's comfort and praise

drains the receiver.

Revealing Manner

Carefully consider

who your true enemy is,

for often,

they roam cloaked

as the familiar wolf

in

sheepskin.

Their venom is

unmistakable

if you watch close,

as disguises will always offer imperfections

large enough to poke a hole,

fostering the emergence

of

a bright light

taking

hold.

Unclouded Vision

A genuine love

shines brighter than nightly stars

for the world to see.

Feeding Negativity

I often wonder

what my soul does

when I am

asleep.

Does it live a double life?

Is that where negative

tendencies

reside?

Spiritual Rest

Daily chaotic lives

cause the need for restful sleep,

repairing mistakes.

Sorrowful

Consider yourself fortunate

if you ever have the chance

to experience crushing shame,

for to acknowledge the emotion

with

sincere regret,

symbolizes the epitome

of

spiritual growth —

one where you

are no longer

the

main attraction.

Love Defined

Love is a

very complex

label,

and it defines

a myriad of

interpersonal

relationships.

There is

much joy

to be had

in knowing,

recognizing,

and embracing

all

forms.

Too Many Socks

I once heard

someone say

that the more

socks

one owns,

the more complicated life becomes.

The

socks

represent the simple things

in life.

The more

socks

that you have,

the more they disappear.

What we have left

are unmatched

left-over

socks

all over the place.

Perhaps,

it is better to own

only a few pairs

and

take care of

them.

The Fox

The larger your clan grows,

the easier it becomes

for the fox to enter

the hen house

and slyly gaze

at the wreckage

about

to unfold.

Exempt by Design

Society has a fault

of never questioning

the gatekeepers

of life.

Said gatekeepers often

are the very ones that create

the rules,

leaving themselves

exempt.

Transparent Rules

Question the status

quo, for everything should be

transparently viewed.

Cognitive Dissonance

Dissonance

is the result

of theory and perception combined

when the

underlying premises

misalign.

Fraudulent

When your whispered words

contradict innate actions,

fraud is the result.

Author News

M. Gail Grant would like to thank her readers and kindly ask you to leave a review on GoodReads and the vendor from which you purchased your book. She is very grateful for your feedback and thoughts for future readers.

MGailGrant.com
Facebook.com/MGailGrant
Twitter.com/MGailGrant
Instagram.com/MGailGrant

Poetry:

Bluebirds and Faith
Elephant Wisdom
Poetic Christian Discourse, Vol. 1

Faith-Based Fantasy Fiction Middle-Grade Series:

Magdalena Gottschalk: The Crooked Trail, Book #1

Magdalena Gottschalk: The Slippery Slope, Book #2

Magdalena Gottschalk: Lindtzl Kingdom, Book #3

Magdalena Gottschalk: The Grand Ball ... *Coming Soon*

Made in the USA
Las Vegas, NV
13 January 2023

65584961R00105